Can You Fly?

Written by Debra Green
Illustrated by Fraser Williamson

"Can you fly?"

"Yes," said the pelican.

"Can you fly?"

"Yes," said the bee.

"Can you fly?"

"Yes," said the parrot.

"Can you fly?"

"Yes," said the butterfly.

"Can you fly?"

"Yes," said the bat.

"Can you fly?"

"Yes," said the sparrow.

"Can you fly?"

"Yes," said Katy.
"I can fly."